IMAGES OF WAR

WAFFEN-SS IN NORMANDY 1944

RARE PHOTOGRAPHS FROM WARTIME ARCHIVES

Ian Baxter

Pen & Sword
MILITARY

First published in Great Britain in 2022 by
PEN & SWORD MILITARY
an imprint of
Pen & Sword Books Ltd
47 Church Street
Barnsley
South Yorkshire
S70 2AS

ISBN 978-1-39909-141-1

A CIP catalogue record for this book is available from the British Library.

Typeset by Concept, Huddersfield, West Yorkshire HD4 5JL
Printed and bound in England by CPI Group (UK) Ltd, Croydon CR0 4YY

FSC www.fsc.org MIX Paper from responsible sources FSC® C013604

Pen & Sword Books Limited incorporates the imprints of Atlas, Archaeology, Aviation, Discovery, Family History, Fiction, History, Maritime, Military, Military Classics, Politics, Select, Transport, True Crime, Air World, Frontline Publishing, Leo Cooper, Remember When, Seaforth Publishing, The Praetorian Press, Wharncliffe Local History, Wharncliffe Transport, Wharncliffe True Crime and White Owl.

For a complete list of Pen & Sword titles please contact
PEN & SWORD BOOKS LIMITED
47 Church Street, Barnsley, South Yorkshire S70 2AS, England
E-mail: enquiries@pen-and-sword.co.uk
Website: www.pen-and-sword.co.uk

Contents

About the Author

Ian Baxter is a military historian who specialises in German twentieth-century military history. He has written more than fifty books including *Poland – The Eighteen Day Victory March, Panzers In North Africa, The Ardennes Offensive, The Western Campaign, The 12th SS Panzer-Division Hitlerjugend, The Waffen-SS on the Western Front, The Waffen-SS on the Eastern Front, The Red Army at Stalingrad, Elite German Forces of World War II, Armoured Warfare, German Tanks of War, Blitzkrieg, Panzer-Divisions at War, Hitler's Panzers, German Armoured Vehicles of World War Two, Last Two Years of the Waffen-SS at War, German Soldier Uniforms and Insignia, German Guns of the Third Reich, Defeat to Retreat: The Last Years of the German Army At War 1943–45, Operation Bagration – the Destruction of Army Group Centre, German Guns of the Third Reich, Rommel and the Afrika Korps, U-Boat War,* and most recently *The Sixth Army and the Road to Stalingrad.* He has written over a hundred articles including 'Last days of Hitler', 'Wolf's Lair', 'The Story of the V1 and V2 Rocket Programme', 'Secret Aircraft of World War Two', 'Rommel at Tobruk', 'Hitler's War With his Generals', 'Secret British Plans to Assassinate Hitler', 'The SS at Arnhem', 'Hitlerjugend', 'Battle of Caen 1944', 'Gebirgsjäger at War', 'Panzer Crews', 'Hitlerjugend Guerrillas', 'Last Battles in the East', 'The Battle of Berlin', and many more. He has also reviewed numerous military studies for publication, supplied thousands of photographs and important documents to various publishers and film production companies worldwide, and lectures to various schools, colleges and universities throughout the United Kingdom and the Republic of Ireland.

Introduction

On 6 June 1944, Operation OVERLORD was regarded as the greatest amphibious invasion in military history. German defences situated along the Normandy coastline quickly crumbled in spite of stiff resistance in some areas. In order to prop up the disintegrating lines, Hitler's only way out from his forces being completely overrun by the Allies was by utilizing his premier Waffen-SS divisions as the backbone for both offensive and defensive operations in the Normandy countryside. What followed was vicious fighting by units such as the *Leibstandarte*, *Das Reich*, *Hitlerjugend*, *Hohenstaufen*, *Frundsberg* and *Götz von Berlichingen* divisions.

This book, with its extensive text and rare and unpublished photographs with detailed captions, tells the story of the Waffen-SS operations in Normandy and their subsequent retreat through France. It describes how these formidable SS units with their supporting Wehrmacht divisions attempted to drive back their enemy, sending their powerful armour along the twisting narrow Normandy roads and across the fields and hedgerows, fanatically fighting to hold almost every village and town as they slowly fell back. However, their forces were steadily ground down by mounting losses and lack of supplies and fuel. Hindered by overwhelming enemy airpower, together with the unyielding resistance of Allied ground forces, it culminated in the loss of the battle of Operation GOODWOOD and the Falaise Pocket, which saw twenty-five out of the thirty-eight German divisions being completely destroyed. As a result, the Waffen-SS were reluctantly withdrawn and the remnants of this foremost fighting machine were transferred back to Holland or Belgium to recoup, or sent to the Eastern Front to deal with another mounting threat.

Chapter One

Prelude to Invasion

Prior to the Allied Normandy invasion in June 1944, the military situation for the German war machine had deteriorated. The first six months of the year for the German soldier were very gloomy. On the Eastern Front they had fought desperately to maintain cohesion and hold their meagre positions that often saw thousands perish. As Waffen-SS and Wehrmacht forces established defensive lines in the face of the advancing enemy, commanders looked to the aggressive and loyal striking force of the SS to be counted on to snatch victory from defeat, but even the elite divisions of the Waffen-SS were severely worn down by constant fighting. Most of these premier Waffen-SS divisions would soon find themselves shifted from the Eastern to the Western Front. The redesignated 1st SS Panzer Division *Leibstandarte SS Adolf Hitler* had been ordered back to Russia in November 1943 where the division saw heavy fighting in the Zhitomir area. Its units were assigned to XLVIII Panzer Corps, a part of 4th Panzer Army, which had lost considerable numbers of men and armour around Zhitomir. By the end of January 1944, the division was pulled out of the line and shifted to the Cherkassy region where it was assigned to III Panzer Corps, part of 1st Army. As part of the Corps, the division became heavily embroiled in fighting to help in the relief attempt of German forces of Army Group South encircled in what was known as the Korsun Pocket. Losses were high and in order to recuperate the bulk of the division, the majority of its units were pulled out of the battle front and withdrawn to Belgium for rest and refit, leaving behind a *Kampfgruppe* to fight on. On 25 March, the 1st Panzer Army became encircled in the Kamenets-Podolsky Pocket. The battlegroup then took part in fighting to escape the encirclement, forming part of the spearhead that linked up with II SS Panzer Corps.

In the West, the *Leibstandarte* Division was quickly re-formed in Belgium and was at full strength by 25 April 1944. However, with growing reports of a possible Allied landing in the Pas-de-Calais area the division was not sent back to Russia. Instead it was transferred again as part of I SS Panzer Corps, which at this time consisted of the 101 SS Heavy Panzer Battalion, SS Division *Hitlerjugend*, known as the 'Baby Division', SS Division *Götz von Berlichingen* and the *Panzer Lehr* Division. It shifted its men and heavy armour north of the River Seine to counter any possible attack in and around Calais.

Another Waffen-SS premier division that would see action on the Western Front in the summer of 1944 was the newly-redesignated *Das Reich* Division. As with the *Leibstandarte*, *Das Reich* saw extensive fighting on the Eastern Front. In January 1944 its units were rushed to the Korsun Pocket, where more than 35,000 Wehrmacht troops had become encircled and were consequently trapped. The SS were determined to wrench open the pocket and allow as many troops as possible to break free. As a result of this sacrifice *Das Reich* suffered heavy casualties, but enabled some 33,000 troops to escape with their lives.

Following the break-out in the Korsun Pocket, *Das Reich* Division, now totally depleted with most of its armour lost in battle, was withdrawn from the front and sent to France for rest and refitting. A *Kampfgruppe* from the *Das Reich* Division under the command of SS-Oberführer Heinz Lammerding remained in southern Russia to continue German attempts to try to hold back the Red Army.

In April 1944, a battered and badly depleted *Das Reich* was withdrawn from the front and sent to the West for a rest and refit. Of the 2,500 soldiers of the *Das Reich Kampfgruppe*, only around 800 soldiers reached Toulouse in the south-west of France to rejoin the rest of their division.

While *Das Reich* recuperated in the warm climate of the south of France, other SS divisions were also pulled out of the front and sent to the West. The 9th SS Panzer Division *Hohenstaufen* that had taken part in the relief operation of German forces trapped in the Kamenets-Podolsky Pocket in March 1944 was ordered back to the West on trains in June. The division had formed into II SS Panzer Corps and saw heavy action near the town of Tarnopol. The division's actions helped prevent the encirclement of the 1st Panzer Army, but it came at a heavy price and during these battles *Hohenstaufen* suffered 1,011 casualties. The division would not see its transfer order to the West until after the Allied invasion when both surviving elements of the division and the powerful II SS Panzer Corps were transported to the Caen area.

The *Hohenstaufen*'s sister formation, the 10th SS Division *Frundsberg*, also saw heavy fighting in the Ukraine. Its first action was at Tarnopol in April 1944 and, like the *Hohenstaufen* Division, it later took part in the relief of German troops cut off in the Kamenets-Podolsky Pocket. Two months later, before the division was completely destroyed, *Frundsberg* was pulled out of line west of the River Bug and ordered to the West in June.

Another Waffen-SS division to be sent to the West was none other than the newly-created 12th SS Panzer Division *Hitlerjugend*. The majority of its junior enlisted men had been drawn from the Hitler Youth, while the senior NCOs and officers were from other Waffen-SS divisions. The division had more than 16,000 recruits on its roster and was fresh and eager to fight. They had been undergoing fierce intensive training at Beverloo Camp in Leopoldsburg, Belgium.

By March 1944 the 12th SS was attached to I SS Panzer Corps and weeks later ordered to Caen in Normandy. At the beginning of June, the division had more than 150 tanks.

The last division to see action in the West was the 17th *SS.Panzergrenadier-Division Götz von Berlichingen*. The division was raised near Poitiers in France as the *Panzer-Grenadier-Division Götz von Berlichingen* in October 1943. It was initially formed from a cadre of replacement units and conscripts, many of whom were Romanian Germans and French volunteers. In January 1944 *Götz von Berlichingen* was placed under LXXX Army Corps, a part of *Generalfeldmarschall* Gerd von Rundstedt's Army Group D. By early 1944 the division was retitled the 17th *SS-Panzer-Grenadier-Division Götz von Berlichingen*. In February 1944 the division still lacked vehicles and began rounding up French vehicles in an attempt to complete its mobilization. By March most of the major combat formations were fully motorized, although two of the six infantry battalions were still on bicycles. By 1 June, *Götz von Berlichingen* was moved to Thouars in France. Although it had no Panzers, there were armoured units fully equipped with the forty-two *Sturmgeschütz* IV assault guns.

SS-Brigadeführer und Generalmajor der Waffen-SS Theodor Wisch. He was a commander of the SS Division *Leibstandarte* (LSSAH) and in this photograph can be seen decorated wearing the Knight's Cross of the Iron Cross with Oak Leaves and Swords. He assumed command of the *Leibstandarte* in April 1943. He was seriously wounded in combat on the Western Front by a naval artillery barrage during the break-out in the Falaise Pocket on 20 August 1944 and replaced as division commander by *SS-Brigadeführer* Wilhelm Mohnke.

(**Above, left**) *SS-Gruppenführer* Heinz Lammerding commanded the SS Panzer Division *Das Reich*. At the end of 1943, he had initially been given command of a battlegroup of *Das Reich* in a partisan combat role. It was not until 25 January 1944 that he was given command of the entire division. He remained in command until he was wounded on 25 July 1944 in Normandy.

(**Above, right**) *SS-Obergruppenführer* Wilhelm Bittrich was given command of the 9th SS Panzer Division *Hohenstaufen* from February 1943 to 1 July 1944. From July 1944 until the end of the war Bittrich then commanded the 2nd SS Panzer Corps in Normandy.

(**Right**) *SS-Brigadeführer* Sylvester Stadler was appointed commander of SS Division *Hohenstaufen* from 10 to 31 July 1944. From 1 March 1942 he had commanded the 2nd Battalion of the Panzer Grenadier Regiment *Der Führer* belonging to the SS Division *Das Reich*. In May 1943 he was appointed commander of the entire *Der Führer* Regiment. A year later when his regiment was called to Normandy the unit under his direct command committed the Oradour-sur-Glane massacre. On 10 July 1944 Stadler was appointed commander of the SS Division *Hohenstaufen* which was sent from the Eastern Front to Normandy.

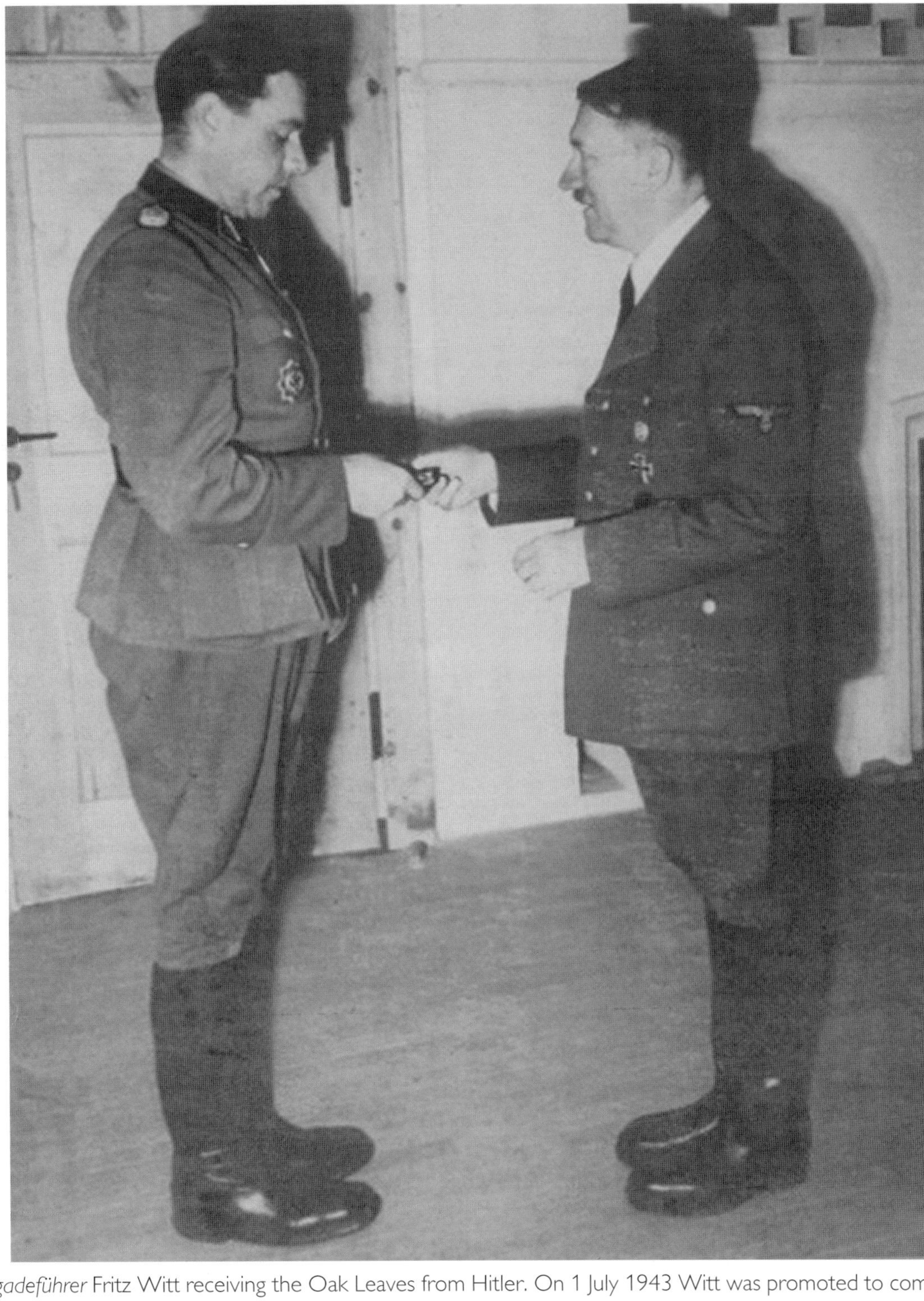

SS-Brigadeführer Fritz Witt receiving the Oak Leaves from Hitler. On 1 July 1943 Witt was promoted to commander of the SS Division *Hitlerjugend* where he oversaw training of the division at the Beverloo camp in Belgium. In March the division was transferred to France in expectation of an Allied invasion. On 20 April 1944 Witt was promoted to *SS-Brigadeführer*. He commanded the *Hitlerjugend* Division for just over a week during the Normandy operation as he was killed in action by a Royal Navy artillery barrage that hit the divisional command post at Venoix. *(Bender)*

(**Above, left**) *SS-Brigadeführer und Generalmajor der Waffen-SS* Heinz Harmel was commander of the 10th SS Panzer Division *Frundsberg*, of which he took command in early 1944. During the early summer the division was moved to the Normandy area.

(**Above, right**) *SS-Brigadeführer und Generalmajor der Waffen-SS* Wilhelm Mohnke. He was appointed to command a regiment in the 12th SS Division *Hitlerjugend* in 1943. He was later to lead the unit in the Battle for Caen and for his tactical brilliance on the battlefield he received the Knight's Cross of the Iron Cross on 11 July 1944. (Bender)

(**Right**) *SS-Obersturmbannführer* Kurt Meyer took command of the 12th SS Panzer Division *Hitlerjugend* following the death of Fritz Witt on 16 June 1944. He was the next highest-ranking officer and was promoted to divisional commander at 33 years of age. He was one of the war's youngest German divisional commanders. On 27 August Meyer was awarded the Swords to the Knight's Cross with Oak Leaves and promoted to *SS-Brigadeführer*. (Bender)

(**Above, left**) *SS-Gruppenführer und Generalleutnant der Waffen-SS* Werner Ostendorff was commander of the 17th SS-Panzergrenadier-Division *Götz von Berlichingen*. His command in Normandy was short-lived as he was seriously wounded. (Bender)

(**Above, right**) *SS-Obersturmbannführer* Otto Baum took temporary command of the 17th SS-Panzergrenadier-Division *Götz von Berlichingen* on 20 June 1944, replacing *SS-Gruppenführer und Generalleutnant der Waffen-SS* Werner Ostendorff who was seriously wounded near Carentan on 16 June 1944. He took command of the SS Division *Das Reich* in July 1944. (Bender)

(**Left**) *SS-Standartenführer* Otto Binge took over temporary command of the 17th SS Panzergrenadier Division *Götz von Berlichingen* between 1 and 30 August 1944. (Bender)

SS-Oberstgruppenführer und Generaloberst der Waffen-SS Sepp Dietrich. Dietrich had been the commander of the *Leibstandarte* throughout the campaigns in both Greece and Yugoslavia before being promoted to command of the 1st SS Panzer Corps on the Eastern Front. He later scored sizable successes in Normandy with the Corps where it was assigned the *Leibstandarte, Hitlerjugend, Panzer-Lehr* and *Götz von Berlichingen* divisions. (Bender)

SS Brigadeführer Fritz Krämer acted as Sepp Dietrich's deputy of the 1st SS Panzer Corps during the battles in Normandy. (Bender)

SS Gruppenführer Wilhelm Bittrich had initially been commander of the 9th SS Panzer Division *Hohenstaufen* from February 1943 to 1 July 1944. He was then immediately appointed commander of II SS Panzer Corps. (Bender)

Panzertruppen of the SS *Leibstandarte* in Belgium in the spring of 1944 during a ceremony. The majority of the LSSAH, which amounted to 41 officers and 1,188 men, were withdrawn from the Eastern Front to Belgium for rest and refit prior to moving to Normandy. *(NARA)*

Three photographs taken in sequence showing *Panzertruppen* of the SS *Leibstandarte* during what appears to be a decoration ceremony in Belgium in the spring of 1944. By 25 April the division was back to full strength, and for operations in Normandy it was transferred again as part of I SS Panzer Corps which comprised 101 SS Heavy Panzer Battalion, SS Division *Hitlerjugend*, SS Division *Götz von Berlichingen* and the *Panzer-Lehr* Division. (NARA)

Officers of *Das Reich* Division conferring while at a training barracks in France in the spring of 1944. The division had been withdrawn from the mud flats of the Eastern Front for a rest and refit before taking part in the defence of southern France. Its units were moved to the town of Montauban, just north of Toulouse. It was here that the divisional staff could prepare their men in a quiet area but stand ready to intervene on the north or south coasts of France when the Allies landed. *(NARA)*

The first of seven photographs taken in sequence showing *Das Reich* soldiers, commanding officers and NCOs at a shooting range while training in France in the spring of 1944. Throughout its period of training the division was continuously interrupted by being ordered to take part in anti-partisan sweeps against French resistance. Week by week, its units had to leave their large encampment of some fifty barracks and lagers and carry out operations in the French countryside. Although these operations were considered a hindrance to the division, as a whole its men were able to carry out intensive training and rebuild their depleted arsenal. Many of the men, especially the hardened veterans of the Eastern Front, were still imbued with a determination to do whatever was required of them that would bring them victory, both against the French resistance and the Allies. *(NARA)*

150

(**Above**) Soldiers of the 9th SS-Panzer-Division *Hohenstaufen* hitching a lift on board a StuG.III while operating on the Eastern Front. The division had taken part in the relief operation of German forces trapped in the Kamenets-Podolsky Pocket in March 1944. Three months later its units found themselves being withdrawn from Russia and ordered back to the West on trains in June for operations in Normandy.

(**Opposite, above**) A well-camouflaged Pz.Kpfw.IV Ausf.G of the 10th Panzer Division *Frundsberg* during operations in Tarnopol in April 1944. Two months later, before the division was completely destroyed, *Frundsberg* was pulled out of line west of the River Bug and ordered to the West in June.

(**Opposite, below**) During what appears to be a decoration ceremony, commanding officers of the 12th SS Panzer Division *Hitlerjugend* can be seen with their men. The majority of the junior enlisted men of the division had been drawn from members of the Hitler Youth, while the senior NCOs and officers were from other Waffen-SS divisions. The division had more than 16,000 recruits on its roster. Prior to operations in Normandy, the division had been undergoing fierce intensive training at Beverloo Camp in Leopoldsburg, Belgium.

Field Marshal Gerd von Rundstedt, Commander-in-Chief West, inspects members of the *Hitlerjugend* Division in February 1944. *(BA, Bender)*

A commanding officer of the *Hitlerjugend* Division can be seen here lecturing *Hitlerjugend* children who can be seen clad in their black uniforms. They watch and listen intently as the officer speaks to them about a career path in the 12th SS Division. In front of the youths are fully-clad SS soldiers wearing their familiar summer SS tunics. *(BA, Bender)*

Two photographs showing newly-recruited *Panzertruppen* of the famous 12th SS Panzer Division *Hitlerjugend* with the Pz.Kpfw.IV in Belgium, probably in early 1944. *(BA, Bender)*

Soldiers of the *Hitlerjugend* 12th SS next to a stationary half-track while training in Belgium in late 1943 or early 1944. (BA/Bender)

Panzertruppen of the 12th SS stand to attention next to their Pz.Kpfw.IV. By March 1944, the 12th SS was attached to I SS Panzer Corps and weeks later ordered to Caen in Normandy. At the beginning of June, the division had more than 150 tanks. (BA, Bender)

A *Sturmgeschütz* IV crewman poses for the camera from the cupola of his assault gun. Painted on the side of the cupola it reads *Götz von Berlichingen* of the 17th SS Panzergrenadier Division. The division was raised near Poitiers in France in October 1943.

(**Opposite, above**) A StuG.IV of the *Götz von Berlichingen* Division is seen here moving through undergrowth, probably during a training exercise in France in the spring of 1944. By 1 June 1944 its units, fully equipped with forty-two *Sturmgeschütz* IVs moved to Thouars in France.

(**Opposite, below**) A Pz.Kpfw.IV crew poses for the camera on the vehicle's 7.5cm barrel. These crewmen belong to I SS Panzer Corps and this photograph was probably taken in Italy where the Corps initially operated in 1943. In April 1944, the Corps was moved to Septeuil to the west of Paris, where it was assigned the *Leibstandarte*, *Hitlerjugend*, *Panzer-Lehr* and *Götz von Berlichingen* divisions. With the launch of Operation OVERLORD the Corps was ordered to Falaise to engage the enemy. *(NARA)*

(**Above**) Two *SS-Untersturmführers* of the *Götz von Berlichingen* Division can be seen here during a training exercise in France in the spring of 1944. Within days of the Normandy amphibious invasion the division was ordered to take part in the effort to reduce the Allied beachhead.

Two Panther crewmen belonging to II SS Panzer Corps can be seen here in the cupola of the tank. Following the Corps' refit in France it was transferred back to Russia before being withdrawn again in mid-June 1944 in order to assist with operations in Normandy. The Corps would not arrive in the area until late June. For operations in Normandy the components of the Corps comprised the 102nd SS Heavy Panzer Battalion, 9th SS *Hohenstaufen* and 10th SS *Frundsberg* divisions. *(NARA)*

A Panther belonging to II SS Panzer Corps, which was initially formed from units of the *Leibstandarte*, *Das Reich* and *Totenkopf* divisions. The Corps saw extensive combat on the Eastern Front in 1943, but by January 1944 it was moved to the area around Alençon in France for a refit. *(NARA)*

Chapter Two

Invasion

On the eve of the Allied invasion of France, four of the ten German armoured divisions in France and Belgium were Waffen-SS. They consisted of the *Leibstandarte*, *Das Reich*, *Hitlerjugend* and *Götz von Berlichingen*. Even by this late period German intelligence could not confirm with any degree of accuracy where the main Allied invasion would take place. As a consequence the bulk of the Waffen-SS divisions were not located in the Normandy sector under command of the 7th Army. The *Leibstandarte* was lying in the area of Bruges in Belgium, where it had been resting since the spring of 1944 and had become part of the high command strategic reserve and was therefore under Hitler's direct control. *Das Reich* was still in the Toulouse area where the level of partisan operations had increased. The new *Hitlerjugend* Division had been transported by rail from Belgium and was moved close to its expected area of action between the Lower Seine and Orne rivers, while the *Götz von Berlichingen* Division was still stationed in Thouars in France.

The *Hitlerjugend* Division was the nearest of all the four Waffen-SS divisions to the actual Allied landing-point. On paper the division had more than 20,000 soldiers deployed for action in Normandy. Although it was short of a number of armoured vehicles, the troops were well-equipped and armed. After nine months of intensive combat training their spirits were high and they were looking forward to the coming action with confidence. *Sturmmann* Jochen Leykauff scribbled in his diary just before the enemy unleashed the greatest amphibious attack in military history:

> Everyone was waiting in great anticipation for the Allied landings. We were all looking forward to our first action. The Allies planned to destroy the so-called 'baby milk division', as they labelled us, but we were not frightened of them. Sometimes we got so excited at the prospects of fighting, we got big-headed. Although we knew our enemy were superior in numbers, we all trusted our commanders who had become hardened in battle. We had known them since our training first began and we had enjoyed seeing them in the mud and firing live ammunition with steel helmets and machine guns. What really frightened us about the coming invasion were the bomber squadrons, which constantly droned above us dropping tons of bombs.

Just hours before the Allied landings began the *Hitlerjugend* divisional headquarters were informed that enemy paratroopers had jumped behind the coastal sector in Normandy. This, it was predicted, was the prelude to the main attack. A couple of hours later all units of the *Hitlerjugend* were made ready and prepared in their alarm positions. Ninety minutes before the Allied landings began, the *Oberkommando der Wehrmacht* (*OKW*) assigned the *Hitlerjugend* to Army Group B. Yet, despite measures, assessments and orders of the German high and supreme command offices on the growing developments of an Allied landing, the *Hitlerjugend* were not released for action. Even when the enemy landed at 0630 hrs, the *OKW* still forbade them from being released but did approve their advance.

During the course of 6 June convoys of trucks and Panzers of the division navigated the congested narrow roadways of Normandy, moving first into the area around Lisieux and then south-west of the city of Caen. During its march the *Hitlerjugend* were constantly strafed by fighters, disrupting the cohesion of many of the marching columns. By the following morning on 7 June, exhausted from more than a day's constant marching, the bulk of the division had moved into the area north of Caen. By this time reports had confirmed that the enemy had managed to break through some parts of the coastal defences and pushed their attack inland. By 0900 hrs *Sturmbannführer* Kurt Meyer, commander of *Panzer Meyer*, a *Kampfgruppe* comprising three battalions of infantry and a considerable number of Pz.Kpfw.IV tanks, had set up his forward command post in the Ardennes abbey. An hour later the first Panzers of the division moved forward into their assembly areas followed by young SS grenadiers wearing their distinctive green, yellow and brown camouflage smocks. Hidden beneath straw and branches, the Panzers trained their powerful 7.5cm gun barrels towards the advancing enemy. From their positions they could make out the stout, olive-green Sherman tanks moving slowly across the front of their *Kampfgruppen* towards the Caen-Bayeux road. Suddenly the Shermans opened fire and the first Panzer erupted in smoke and flames. Others were also hit and set ablaze by Canadian anti-tank guns. From their hideouts and freshly-dug trenches, the youths crashed into action, opening up a ferocious barrage of fire on British and Canadian positions. At times the fighting was at close quarters, the boys pitching grenades and pumping machine-gun fire into the enemy lines. Although the continuous attack from the air disrupted the grenadiers' assault, the teenagers of the newly-created 12th SS fought on. In the nearby village of Malon, the boys were feverishly taking up positions, stalking the enemy tanks with their deadly *Panzerfaust* and destroying several of them. In total the grenadiers knocked out twenty-eight enemy tanks with a loss of six of their own. Many of the Allied soldiers were shocked at seeing teenagers in SS uniforms. It was their first encounter with the *Hitlerjugend* generation. For months prior to the invasion of Normandy the Allies had ridiculed the *Hitlerjugend* as the 'baby division', but to the soldiers that fought against these youngsters, this was far from being a division of badly-trained teenagers.

Testimony of their fighting skills and endurance on the battlefield clearly showed during the initial stages of the Allied invasion as they were the only premier division in Normandy. The *Leibstandarte* was still waiting for the predicted main attack from the Allies in the Calais region. *Das Reich* was still in Toulouse, and *Hohenstaufen* had been withdrawn in April and early May to act as a mobile reserve for Army Group North Ukraine in anticipation of a renewed Russian offensive. By the time of the Allied invasion in the West the division was still refitting in the Ukraine. It would not be until around 11 June that *Hohenstaufen* would receive new orders and begin entraining their equipment for a movement back to France. The order signed by Field Marshal Model remarked: 'I am certain that you will accomplish your new missions in the spirit of our slogan "No soldier in the world is better than the soldiers of Adolf Hitler!"' As for its sister division *Frundsberg*, it had been fighting in Poland, west of the River Bug in a static position. As the Allies invaded the Normandy beaches *Frundsberg* received no orders for almost a week. It was not until 12 June along with II SS Panzer Corps that it would finally be withdrawn from the Eastern Front and rushed west to respond to the Normandy landings. Its personnel and equipment were immense, filling some sixty-seven trains bound for the Western Front. As for the *Götz von Berlichingen* Division, its units were ordered to Normandy on 7 June. However, because its units were still in Tours/Angers, coupled with the lack of transport it would be weeks away from supporting defensive operations in Normandy.

With no premier Waffen-SS divisions in the Normandy area it was left to the *Hitlerjugend*. Over the next few days, as the battle intensified, the *Hitlerjugend* came under even heavier attacks. Still this did not encourage the grenadiers to be driven from their bombed and blasted positions for they had been given orders to hold the enemy at all costs and prevent them from penetrating their lines and breaking through to the ancient city of Caen.

During the evening of 9 June the *Panzer-Lehr* Division moved into line alongside the 12th SS after travellng miles to the front from Chartres. The following day the 21st Panzer Division also moved up and helped the other two divisions form the principal shield around Caen, with motley other ad hoc units that had retreated from the coastal sector. During the days and weeks that followed, the *Hitlerjugend*, *Lehr* Division and the 21st Panzer carried on fighting superbly in and around the city of Caen, which was slowly being reduced to rubble. All day and night the fighting raged. Many soldiers were killed at point-blank range, while others fighting in the hedgerows and ditches fought to the death. Through the lanes and farm tracks that crisscrossed the Normandy countryside, rows of dead from both sides lay sprawled out amid a mass of hand grenades and smashed and burned-out vehicles.

The *Hitlerjugend* had been fighting continuously and the German high command was aware of the growing problems that were manifest along the battered front. With the other premier SS divisions preparing to rush to assist the deteriorating situation near Beauvais, north-west of Paris, the 101st Heavy SS Panzer Battalion or *Schwere SS-Panzerabteilung* 101 was ordered to Normandy. Of its forty-five Tigers, thirty-seven were operational and the remaining eight were still under repair. On 8 June the 101st moved from its training area. The 1st and 2nd *Schwere SS-Panzerabteilung* 101 marched via Verneul-l'Aigle, while the 1st *Schwere SS-Panzerabteilung* 101 proceeded to drive via Vimoutiers to the area south of Caen. The 2nd *Schwere SS-Panzerabteilung* 101 moved via Argentan to Falaise. The 3rd *Schwere SS-Panzerabteilung* 101 was compelled to return to Paris and commenced single tank movement to the West the next day due to heavy enemy strafing attacks by fighter-bombers. During the next few days, road marches were conducted only during the night due to the Allied air threat. On 10 June the 2nd *Schwere SS-Panzerabteilung* 101 was strafed by fighters in Argentan. A short while later it was hit again from the air at Occagnes. One aircraft was shot down by *SS-Unterscharführer* Warmbrunn with anti-aircraft machine-gun fire. The 2nd *Schwere SS-Panzerabteilung* 101 arrived in Falaise during the night of 9 June. During the night, the battalion completed its arrival in its designated assembly area, experiencing many mechanical problems and failures during the road march. The 1st *Schwere SS-Panzerabteilung* 101 with eight Tigers assembled north-east of Villers-Bocage, while the 2nd *Schwere SS-Panzerabteilung* 101 with six Tigers moved south of Montbrocq. The battalion was then immediately ordered to cover the left flank of the newly-arrived I SS Panzer Corps because of heavy naval shelling.

In April 1944, I SS Panzer Corps had been moved to Septeuil to the west of Paris. When the invasion was launched the Corps received orders to rush to Normandy. Although it was attached to 5th Panzer, the Western theatre's armoured reserve, it would be released immediately and would see extensive action. It was assigned to the *Hitlerjugend* and *Panzer-Lehr* Division, but over the coming weeks when more premier divisions arrived it was also assigned to the *Leibstandarte* and *Götz von Berlichingen* divisions.

(**Opposite**) Two photographs taken by German coastal defence troops showing a stretch of the Normandy beaches. It shows wooden posts or *Hemmbalken* ('obstruction beams') that were planted at an angle in the sand and supported and reinforced by other wooden poles to make them more secure. These were often topped by Teller mines. Due to these sea defences the Allies opted for a low-tide rather than a high-tide landing to avoid damage to their landing craft and high casualty rates. (Bender)

(**Above**) A German coastal soldier emerging from his bunker. In the Normandy region Field Marshal Rommel, who commanded Army Group B, stationed the 91st, 243rd, 352nd, 709th, 711th and 716th infantry divisions, together with the 6th *Fallschirmjäger* Regiment, the 30th Mobile Brigade and the Russian *Buniatchenko* Brigade. When the Allied invasion came there were three Panzer divisions within striking distance, but not one of them was ordered to the invasion beaches. Instead, the German 352nd Infantry Division at Omaha Beach, the 709th Static Division at Utah and the 716th Static Division at Gold, Juno and Sword Beaches were left to try to repel the Allies. Many of the troops that were employed for coastal defences had hardly any battle experience or proper training. Yet, despite being poorly-organized and lacking sufficient weapons, they were dedicated to delaying the advance of the Allies and preventing them from obtaining a foothold along the beaches.

(**Opposite, above**) Coastal Luftwaffe FlaK troops during a training exercise prior to the invasion with their 8.8cm FlaK gun. Apart from FlaK batteries spread along the coastal area, the Germans had constructed coastal artillery batteries under the control of either the army or the navy. These were spaced several miles apart and were designed to fire out to sea and ward off any invasion fleet. They were equipped with guns that were generally grouped in fours or – more rarely – in sixes.

(**Opposite, below**) An SS FlaKman is seen here looking through a pair of 10x80 Doppelfernrohr Double Telescope FlaK artillery binoculars during operations in Normandy in June. These binoculars were probably being used in conjunction with the 8.8cm FlaK gun for firing ranges.

(**Above**) A stationary StuG.III Ausf.G can be seen here on a road. The crewmen can be seen conversing with other assault gun crews before resuming their drive. Note the foliage attached to the vehicle in order to help break up its distinctive shape against both aerial and ground recognition.

(**Opposite, above**) An MG 34 coastal defence gun crew can be seen here with their weapon bolted on a Lafette tripod, which is mounted with a telescopic gun sight. The coastal defences in the Normandy area were soon overwhelmed by Allied superiority in spite of the huge losses inflicted on the American forces on Omaha Beach.

(**Opposite, below**) An Sd.Kfz.251 from the 12th SS Panzer Division *Hitlerjugend* advances along a road bound for the front, probably in the Caen area. The *Hitlerjugend* Division was the nearest of all the four Waffen-SS divisions to the actual Allied landing-point. *(Bender)*

A well-concealed Sd.Kfz.251 half-track can be seen here with a *Hitlerjugend* grenadier inside. During the Battle of Normandy the *Hitlerjugend* continued to fight on for days and weeks. For four weeks they battled without relief and as a consequence suffered huge losses in both men and equipment. By mid-July 1944 the division had suffered 60 per cent casualties, a third of whom were killed.

Here a *Hitlerjugend* soldier is about to dismount from an Sd.Kfz.251 half-track and go into action. Despite its severe mauling by Allied bombing, the 12th SS Division was far from beaten and fought on courageously. All over the Normandy sector the division desperately continued trying to keep the Allies in check. The Normandy countryside had created conditions that favoured the SS grenadiers. Clusters of trees, tall hedges, ditches and lack of roads frustrated the Allied armoured units seeking to destroy enemy tanks in open areas. Aided by this terrain, the SS were able to defend positions longer than the Allies had expected possible and as a result they incurred huge casualties. Frequently the Allies watched their irrepressible foe come under a furious crescendo of mortar and shellfire and still they held their ground to the grim death. However, savage Allied air attacks and naval bombardments gradually began to grind down the German defences. Movement was almost impossible by daylight and any vehicles that travelled during the day were attacked and destroyed.

A *Hitlerjugend* soldier can be seen here sitting on the roof of a vehicle prior to continuing the unit's march into action.

Hitlerjugend soldiers can be seen here on the march. By the following morning on 7 June, exhausted from more than a day's constant marching, the bulk of the 12th SS had moved into the area north of Caen. By this time reports had confirmed that the enemy had managed to break through some parts of the coastal defences and had pushed their attack inland.

Two *Hitlerjugend* soldiers converse. For months prior to the invasion of Normandy, the Allies had ridiculed the *Hitlerjugend* as the 'baby division', but to the soldiers that fought against the 12th SS, this was far from a division of badly-trained teenagers. It was an elite division that inspired fear and, at the same time, fought a battle that inspired even its enemies. In front of Caen soldiers of the *Hitlerjugend* took up positions, stalking the enemy tanks with their deadly *Panzerfaust* and destroying several of them. Many of the Allied soldiers were shocked at seeing teenagers in SS uniforms. It was their first encounter with the *Hitlerjugend* generation.

A well-concealed machine-gunner watches some of his comrades returning after a reconnaissance patrol. The MG 42 is mounted on a sustained fire mount. All the grenadiers can be seen armed with a 9mm MP 38/40 machine pistol, one of the most effective submachine guns ever produced. The MP 38/40 machine pistol was commonly called the 'Schmeisser' by the Allies after its designer of the same name.

A *Hitlerjugend* grenadier can be seen here well concealed in a foxhole armed with the Karabiner 98k bolt-action rifle and an M1924 stick grenade.

A Pz.Kpfw.IV Ausf.H belonging to the 12th SS Panzer Division of SS Panzer Regiment 12 is seen here on the march through a French town in June. *(Bender)*

An assault gun crewman of the *Götz von Berlichingen* Division seen posing for the camera with a cat during a halt on its march to Normandy.

A young Pz.Kpfw.IV crewman belonging to the 12th SS Division Panzer Regiment is seen here standing next to his vehicle during a lull in the fighting.

SS-Sturmbannführer Fritz Witt, *SS-Obersturmbannführer* Max Wünsche and *SS-Sturmbannführer* Kurt Meyer of the 12th SS Panzer Division *Hitlerjugend* at the Ardennes abbey near Caen in June. On 14 June Witt was killed when a naval barrage hit his command post. Meyer, the next highest-ranking officer, was promoted to divisional commander. (*BA/Bender*)

SS-Obersturmbannführer Max Wünsche (left), *SS-Sturmbannführer* Fritz Witt (centre) and *SS-Sturmbannführer* Kurt Meyer (right) taken near Caen between 7 and 13 June. (*BA/Bender*)

(**Above**) SS grenadiers of the 9th *Hohenstaufen* Division resting along a road during operations near Caen in June. The division could do little more than fight defensive actions, and over the coming days its units were thrown into vicious fighting around Caen including bloody combat to seize and hold the critically important heights along Hill 112.

(**Opposite, above**) Soldiers are seen here conversing next to a stationary Kübelwagen 82. Along the road a column of vehicles are on fire, obviously destroyed by an aerial attack.

(**Opposite, below**) SS grenadiers belonging to the 12th SS seen removing a barbed-wire entanglement from across a road in the Caen area.

An SS soldier can be seen here in a defensive position armed with the MP 40. While the SS excelled at offensive operations, by this point in the war they had learned the art of tactical defence.

An assault gun crewman holding the rank of an *SS-Standartenjunker* is seen with his *Sturmgeschütz*. The 7.5cm gun barrel has been camouflaged. The soldier's rank was a special position held by those aspiring to officer commissions in the Waffen-SS.

A 15cm gun crew during a fire mission against an enemy target.

Two photographs taken in sequence showing *SS-Sturmbannführer* Heinz von Westernhagen clad in camouflage uniform seen near Beauvais in May 1944 prior to the *Schwere SS-Panzerabteilung* 101 being sent to Normandy with its powerful Tigers. Westernhagen was battalion commander. By early June the battalion marched from Paris on to Falaise through Dreux, Verneuil and Argentan. *(Bender)*

A Tiger tank belonging to the Heavy SS Panzer Battalion or *Schwere SS-Panzerabteilung* 101 heading towards Normandy. Note the Type 166 *Schwimmwagen*. The battalion was stationed near Beauvais, north-west of Paris, and was ordered to Normandy. Of its forty-five Tigers, thirty-seven were operational and the remaining eight were still under repair. On 8 June the 101st moved from its training area. The 1st and 2nd *Schwere SS-Panzerabteilung* 101 marched via Verneuil-l'Aigle, while the 1st *Schwere SS-Panzerabteilung* 101 proceeded to drive via Vimoutiers to the area south of Caen. *(Bender)*

(**Opposite, above**) A Tiger from *Schwere SS-Panzerabteilung* 101 negotiating one of the narrow roads in a French town in June. Once the battalion had arrived in Normandy, the 1st *Schwere SS-Panzerabteilung* 101 with eight Tigers assembled north-east of Villers-Bocage, while the 2nd *Schwere SS-Panzerabteilung* 101 with six Tigers moved south of Montbrocq.

(**Above**) A Tiger tank belonging to *Schwere SS-Panzerabteilung* 101 has halted here on a road inside a Normandy town in June.

(**Opposite, below**) Tiger 131 of *Schwere SS-Panzerabteilung* 101. The road march to Normandy had been difficult for the battalion with various mechanical breakdowns and air attacks. The battalion moved to Normandy near Caen on 12 June. The next day elements of *2.Kompanie* halted the British advance on Caen in the Battle of Villers-Bocage. *(Bender)*

In a defensive position here is an MG 42 heavy machine gun on the sustained fire mount. This lethal weapon was, in 1944, regarded as more than enough to keep open the flanks for attacking infantry. Many successful engagements were made by the SS using both the MG 34 and MG 42 machine guns.

Chapter Three

Bitter Fighting

After a week of combat in Normandy the Germans had shown themselves to be masters of defence, but it came with a heavy cost both in men and matériel. The men had found that battles in Normandy were very different to those fought on the German Eastern Front. Both the Wehrmacht and Waffen-SS were facing many new challenges. The terrain was often crisscrossed with fields surrounded by thick hedgerows and was called the bocage. This meant that countryside severely restricted the manoeuvre of tanks and armoured vehicles, limiting their fields of fire. The terrain also had limited protection and concealment from Allied fighter-bombers which dominated the skies over Normandy. SS soldiers called the fighting *Materialschlacht* in which they were subjected not only to heavy naval fire but overwhelming tanks, fully motorized infantry, superior artillery and damaging attacks from the air.

Although the bulk of the premier SS divisions had still not arrived, those that were operating in northern France were stretched along the front supported by Wehrmacht, *Fallschirmjäger* and Luftwaffe divisions. Operating at intervals, Pz.Kpfw.IVs, Tigers, Panther tanks and a number of StuG.III assault guns, Hetzer and Marder tank destroyers formed a defensive belt and were used sporadically in both defensive and offensive operations. Every possible anti-tank weapon and artillery piece would be used to ambush Allied tanks, while special engineer mobile detachments equipped with anti-personnel and anti-tank mines would quickly deploy and erect new obstacles. Behind these defensive positions at varying depths were crude anti-tank defences, but these included mortars, *Panzerschreck*, *Panzerfaust*, 7.5cm and 8.8cm PaK guns, ready to counter any enemy armoured vehicle that managed to break through.

However, while it appeared that the Germans were prepared along the hedgerows and fields, much of the equipment employed along the defensive belts was too thinly spread. Yet along these thinly-defended parts of the front elite units of the SS showed how tenaciously and brutally they could fight.

The *Götz von Berlichingen* Division which had now made its way into Normandy soon showed how violent it could be on the battlefield. In the village of Graignes heavy fighting broke out on 10 June between the 507th *Fallschirmjäger* and the

82nd American Airborne. The *Götz von Berlichingen* with a regiment-sized force of approximately 2,000 men attacked the village against 182 paratroopers. Outnumbered and fearing complete annihilation, the American paratroopers quickly surrendered. SS troops forced Captain Sophian, his two medics and fourteen wounded paratroopers to line up against a wall where they were divided into two groups and subsequently murdered. One group of five wounded was taken to the edge of a nearby pond where SS troops bayoneted them, throwing their lifeless bodies into the water. The other group of nine was forced to march at gunpoint a couple of miles to a field near the village of Le Mesnil-Angot. After arriving at the field, the group was forced to dig a pit where the SS shot each of the wounded men through the head and pushed their bodies into the pit. Later that same day Captain Sophian and his two medics were also killed by the SS. After the murder other German soldiers began rounding up French civilians suspected of assisting US troops. A total of forty-four villagers were rounded up, interrogated by the Germans as suspected collaborators and then murdered. Other SS men dragged two priests out from the rectory where they were hiding and shot them both dead in the courtyard. The Germans then discovered Madeleine Pezeril and the 80-year-old Eugénie Dujardin and shot them both dead in their beds. After the massacres, the SS then ransacked the village for any valuables they could steal and then set light to the houses on 13 June.

Elsewhere other SS units, notably the *Schwere SS-Panzerabteilung* 101 with its powerful Tigers were assembling north-east of Villers-Bocage on the morning of 13 June. In the area was a detachment of the British 22nd Armoured Brigade advancing along the road attempting to exploit a gap between the 352nd Infantry Division and the *Panzer-Lehr* Division. The Panzer ace *SS-Obersturmführer* Wittmann attacked the British armoured formation comprising the 4th City of London Yeomanry and parts of the 1st Battalion of the Rifle Brigade ahead of its company. He then advanced towards Villers-Bocage destroying two Sherman artillery observer tanks, thirteen M-3 half-tracks, a dozen Bren and Lloyd carriers, three Stuart light tanks, a Daimler scout car of the brigade's intelligence officer and the M-3 of the brigade surgeon. On the outskirts of the town, three of the four Cromwells of the regimental headquarters section of the City of London Yeomanry were destroyed by the Tiger. The tank then rumbled into Villers-Bocage, but Wittmann's advance was halted by enemy tanks. He then withdrew, knocking out a Cromwell in the process, but then was knocked out by enemy anti-tank fire. The crew bailed out of the smoking Tiger and made their way through to the command post of the *Panzer-Lehr* Division at Orbois-Sermentot. The remaining tanks of the 2nd *Schwere SS-Panzerabteilung* 101 occupied positions east of Villers-Bocage and knocked out two more Cromwells and three Shermans. Some 230 British soldiers surrendered and were taken prisoner. Eight Tigers of the 1st *Schwere SS-Panzerabteilung* 101 commanded by *SS-Hauptsturmführer* Möbius then attacked Villers-Bocage including a number of Pz.Kpfw.IVs of the *Panzer-Lehr* Division.

Over the course of several hours, 1st, 2nd and 3rd *Schwere SS-Panzerabteilung* 101 lost three tank commanders and seven other crew members. Three Tigers of the 1st *Schwere SS-Panzerabteilung* 101 were lost, but the British lost eight Bren carriers, fourteen M-3s and twenty-six tanks. In total forty-two enemy tanks were lost. For his skill and tenacity on the battlefield *SS-Obersturmführer* Wittmann was recommended for the Swords to his Knight's Cross.

Elsewhere in the Normandy sector other SS units, notably the 12th SS *Hitlerjugend*, were also scoring sizable hits against the enemy. At Le Mesnil-Patry where the 3rd Canadian Division were positioned the 12th inflicted heavy casualties of the lines against the Queen's Own Rifles of Canada and the 1st Hussars (6th Armoured Regiment) which lost fifty-one Sherman tanks during the battle.

However, a couple of days later on 14 June the commander of the 12th SS, *Brigadeführer* Fritz Witt, was killed at his divisional command post in Venoix, near Caen. This came as a shock to the division. Witt was immediately replaced by Kurt Meyer. At only 33 years old, with the Iron Cross, First and Second Class and the Knight's Cross with Oak Leaves, Meyer was the youngest divisional commander in the German armed forces. Out on the battlefield he was a daredevil commander of unorthodox methods and fought his battles deep inside enemy lines. Yet despite his skill and courageous character the change of command in the 12th SS made no tactical difference. In fact, he took command of the division with it being on the edge of disaster, in spite of a number of successful engagements. Fighting for the defence of Caen had continued with massive losses, despite the preparation of new defences to prevent an enemy offensive on the city.

Troops boarding an infantry transport truck bound for the front.

Two photographs taken in sequence showing soldiers of *Das Reich* Division arresting suspected partisans during their advance through France to Normandy. Just two days after the Allied invasion of northern France, some 15,000 soldiers and 209 Panzers and self-propelled guns began pulling out of the town of Montauban in southern France to begin an arduous northward march across 450 miles of French countryside towards the shores of Normandy. The division's march through France was bathed in blood. During various parts of their drive to Normandy units were hounded by members of the French resistance movement and agents of the Allied Special Forces. What followed was a series of savage reprisals that were some of the most appalling atrocities ever committed during the Second World War. When the Allies unleashed Operation OVERLORD, British intelligence assumed that the *Das Reich* Division would quickly be sent to the Normandy battlefront by at least 10 June. Even the majority of commanders of the division expected to see action within days. In fact, the soldiers had been waiting to entrain for a move 450 miles north to support a counteroffensive that was expected somewhere in northern France. Yet when the Allied landings finally did come, no orders were issued from Army Group G to *Das Reich*. It was not until late on the following day on 7 June that signals were dispatched to all units of *Das Reich*, warning them to prepare for the long journey to the Normandy sector. Despite the fact that the division was not needed urgently at first, all unit commanders were summoned for a conference at *SS-Brigadeführer* Heinz Bernard Lammerding's headquarters on the edge of Montauban. For the commanders of *Das Reich*, movement created huge logistical problems. Armour, for instance, had to be moved over long distances either by rail or transporter. What made problems even worse was that requisitioned French vehicles, sufficient to move entire battalions, had never actually materialized, so the troops had to improvise very quickly. Over the next twenty-four hours, the planning became immensely complex, especially moving out some 15,000 soldiers and more than 1,350 vehicles in march order.

Three photographs taken in 2020 showing the destroyed French town of Oradour-sur-Glane, now a memorial to those that were murdered there. In June 1944, *Das Reich* commanders decided it was time to teach the local population 'what it meant to collaborate with the Resistance'. One such village chosen during *Das Reich*'s drive north to Normandy was Oradour-sur-Glane. It was in this village that *SS-Sturmbannführer* Adolf Diekmann's battalion decided to unleash a bloodbath of vengeance. On the afternoon of 10 June, the population of some 650 watched as Diekmann's armour poured up the main street. With horror, the village folk witnessed camouflage-smocked infantry of the SS fan out through the village firing wildly into the air, shouting and screaming at the civilians and dragging families out into the street. By about 2.25pm, the entire population of Oradour, except for those still hiding like the old and sick, were dragged away and assembled in the Championship de Foire, the little central square. Men and women were separated: men on one side of the square and women and children on the other. Mothers and their children were herded into the church. The men were ordered to face the walls of the house flanking the square and then were led away to a group of barns and garages. Once assembled, the soldiers then opened fire and shot the men in the legs. As they fell to the ground, they were doused in fuel and set alight. The buildings were then burned. Subsequently the soldiers ran from house to house, starting other fires. *(Oradour-sur-Glane Memorial Museum)*

(**Opposite**) The remains of the church at Oradour-sur-Glane today. It was here that more than 400 women and children had been crammed into the building by the SS and massacred. A detonation fuse full of explosives was lit inside the church at the intersection of the nave and chancel. Outside the church, other soldiers prepared themselves for the massacre. With machine guns and rifles loaded and stick grenades at the ready, the soldiers were given the order to hurl grenades into the church and fire into the great throng of women, children and babies. When the church door suddenly swung open, as mothers tried desperately to escape the slaughter, the SS men surged forward, firing wildly as they came. Those crouching at the doorway were machine-gunned and kicked back into the church. Soldiers continued shooting at random. Prams, chairs and masonry were riddled with bullet holes. The corpses were then covered with straw and the badly injured were finished off. Within a matter of minutes, the entire church became a raging inferno. Next morning, Diekmann's men left Oradour, their armoured vehicles loaded with loot. The next day on 12 June, a Wehrmacht convoy drove into Oradour and were appalled by the carnage and death that their SS counterparts had inflicted on the people of the town. As a mark of respect, they dug two huge graves and carried some of the charred remains to their resting-place. Later that afternoon they left, taking with them some livestock. *(Oradour-sur-Glane Memorial Museum)*

(**Above**) Photographed from a tank, soldiers and Panzers can be seen spread out across a field during their advance.

Soldiers of the *Das Reich* Division resting during their march. Resistance against the division as it drove towards Normandy ended at Bella, near Poitiers. However, partisan warfare had not been effectively extinguished in the area. The division arrived exhausted in the rear areas of the battlefront between 15 and 30 June, almost three weeks behind schedule. The units were not inserted into the battle line until 10 July, by which time they had already suffered heavy losses. Despite its severe mauling by Allied bombing, the division was far from beaten but its reputation would now forever be associated with the atrocities of Oradour and Tulle. Within a few days, *Das Reich* was on the move once more, making a determined drive northwards. Resistance against the division ended at Bella, near Poitiers.

A Panzer crewman is seen here looking at a knocked-out Pz.Kpfw.IV during bitter fighting in Villers-Bocage. It was in this area that *Schwere SS-Panzerabteilung* 101 with its powerful Tigers had assembled north-east of Villers-Bocage on the morning of 13 June. In the area was a detachment of the British 22nd Armoured Brigade advancing along the road attempting to exploit a gap between the 352nd Infantry Division and the *Panzer-Lehr* Division. (Bender)

Two Pz.Kpfw.IV Ausf.J variants belonging to the 12th SS *Hitlerjugend* of Panzer Regiment 12 halted in a field during operations in June. Approximately half the Panzer losses in Normandy were total; the rest were being repaired.

A young decorated soldier of the *Hitlerjugend*. Over the next days and weeks as the Battle of Normandy intensified, *Hitlerjugend* units came under even heavier attacks. Yet this still did not discourage these young grenadiers from being driven from their bombed and blasted positions, for they had been given orders to hold the enemy at all costs and prevent them from penetrating their lines.

An SS PaK crew in action against an enemy target in a field.

A *Hitlerjugend* grenadier tucking into his rations during a lull in the fighting.

A *Hitlerjugend* MG42 machine-gunner is seen here resting on a road. Severe losses, especially of Panzergrenadiers and of matériel, were quickly mounting. The losses to 24 June had amounted to 2,550 men.

An SS grenadier can be seen advancing through foliage using bocage as cover. Although the SS and their Wehrmacht counterparts used bocage to their advantage, they also used sunken Norman country lanes to implement strong points and defences in order to stop British and American troops.

A famous photograph taken near Rots on 9 June 1944 of the 18-year-old SS soldier Otto Funk who was part of the *15.Kompanie* SS Panzergrenadier 25 of the 12th SS Panzer Division.

A young *Hitlerjugend* leader of an MG squad just before an attack. An ammunition belt can be seen around his neck, plus a spade attached to his chest. Note the drum magazine on the MG 42 machine gun used for firing from a standing position. (*Bender*)

A Panzergrenadier can be seen here standing next to a Tiger tank belonging to *Schwere SS-Panzerabteilung* 101 near Villers-Bocage in mid-June. The Germans attacked the town and were repulsed, losing several Tigers and Pz.Kpfw.IVs. *(BA/Bender)*

(**Above**) An interesting photograph showing an MG 42 machine-gunner using the shoulder of his No. 2 to maintain accurate firing against an enemy target. In battle conditions in open terrain like this the MG 42 machine-gun squad would often use a sustained fire mount to protect the flanks of the advancing rifle companies. However, in built-up areas or when marching quickly across open ground from one position to another, the crews frequently had to improvise with their machine guns.

(**Opposite, above**) Waffen-SS and *Fallschirmjäger truppen* are seen here assisting an injured soldier following heavy action in a town.

(**Opposite, below**) *SS-Hauptsturmführer* Michael Wittmann can be seen here standing in the turret of his Tiger tank belonging to *Schwere SS-Panzerabteilung* 101 as it negotiates a narrow road en route to Morgny. This battalion was assigned to I SS Panzer Corps and was never permanently attached to any division or regiment. Wittmann was appointed commander of the battalion's second company. *(Bender)*

205

Here concealed in the undergrowth is a Tiger 222 belonging to the 2nd Battalion of *Schwere SS-Panzerabteilung* 101. *SS-Hauptsturmführer* Wittmann is standing in the turret of this vehicle. The photograph was taken prior to the Battle for Villers-Bocage, which commenced on 13 June. The village was crucial for establishing a foothold in the area, with the intended target zone of Hill 213 near the main crossroads to the north of the town. It was Wittmann's idea to deploy Tigers to the area to gain control. *(BA/Bender)*

A Panzer crew can be seen here in front of their Tiger in June and one of the crew members is jokingly holding a wicker casket more than likely containing wine. *(BA/Bender)*

A vehicle belonging to an unidentified unit of *Das Reich* is seen here concealed in undergrowth. Saplings have been draped over the vehicle in order to camouflage it from both aerial and ground recognition.

(**Above**) A decorated Panzer commander belonging to II SS Panzer Corps poses for the camera. It was not until 12 June that II SS Panzer Corps would finally be withdrawn from the Eastern Front and rushed west to respond to the Normandy landings. *(NARA)*

(**Opposite, above**) Grenadiers belonging to II SS Panzer Corps. It was not until 23 June that II SS finally arrived in the Normandy sector with the *Hohenstaufen* Division and its sister division, the 10th SS *Frundsberg*. *(NARA)*

(**Opposite, below**) Two photographs showing Panther crewmen belonging to an unidentified battalion of II SS Panzer Corps servicing an MG 34 on the tank. The Panther typically had two MG 34 armoured fighting vehicle variant machine guns featuring an armoured barrel sleeve. An MG 34 was located co-axially with the main gun on the gun mantlet, and an identical MG 34 was located on the glacis plate and fired by the radio-operator. *(NARA)*

(**Opposite, above**) A photo of a Panther driver in the hull of the vehicle. During operations in June, there were initially only two Panther-equipped Panzer regiments on the Western Front, with a total of 156 Panthers between them. However, according to a status report at the end of July, from June through to August an additional seven Panther regiments were sent into France, reaching a maximum strength of 432. *(NARA)*

(**Opposite, below**) Two photographs taken in sequence showing a Panther crewman belonging to an unidentified Panther battalion of II SS Panzer Corps seen with shells, preparing to stock the vehicle for an operation. All the ammunition for the main armament was stored in the hull, with a considerable amount stored in the sponsons. *(NARA)*

(**Above**) Two Panzer commanders converse next to their tank during operations on the Western Front.

Chapter Four

Final Divisions Arrive

On 20 June Field Marshal Erwin Rommel, the commander of Army Group B received a Führer order to launch a counteroffensive against the Allies between the towns of Caumont-l'Éventé and Saint-Lo. The main objective was to cut a corridor between the American and British armies by recapturing the city of Bayeux and advancing along to the coast. For this operation four SS Panzer divisions and one *Heer* Panzer Division were assigned to the objective. Their assault was to be spearheaded by II SS Panzer comprising the 9th SS Panzer Division *Hohenstaufen* and the 10th SS *Frundsberg*. The 1st *Leibstandarte* and the 2nd SS *Das Reich* would support the attack. The *Das Reich* Division had journeyed from Toulouse in the south of France and had been seriously delayed in reaching the Normandy sector by partisan activity and constant aerial attacks. The convoys of the division had been unable to carry out daylight movement and had crawled northwards through the darkness. All the Panzer divisions that arrived in the Normandy sector were in such bad shape that they needed days to regroup before going into action. German wireless signals were continuously jammed with Panzer commanders requesting fuel, transportation, new routings and other important material needed to sustain their drive. *Das Reich* division was no exception. It arrived exhausted in the rear areas of the battlefront between 15 and 30 June, almost three weeks behind schedule.

As for the *Leibstandarte*, it did not arrive until the night of 27/28 June with the whole division taking another week to group. Most of the tanks used by these formations were Panthers, Tigers and StuG.IIIs.

It was not until 23 June that the *Hohenstaufen* Division finally arrived in the Normandy sector with II SS Panzer Corps and its sister division, the 10th SS *Frundsberg*. Originally, the Corps was to counterattack the British and Americans near Bayeux in order to drive a wedge between the two armies. For this planned counterattack, the Heavy *SS-Panzerabteilung* 102 arrived to support II SS Panzer Corps. The unit was heavily supported by the Tiger. However, the planned counterattack never materialized. Allied forces had thrown German units into disarray and grenadiers of the 9th SS *Hohenstaufen* could do little more than fight defensive actions. Over the coming days the division was thrown into vicious fighting around the city of Caen including bloody combat to seize the critically important heights along Hill 112.

British forces were determined to take Caen. On the morning of 26 June, they finally unleashed a large-scale attack on Caen code-named Operation EPSOM. During the day's fighting at least fifty enemy tanks were knocked out by the Panzers and PaK guns alone. The 12th SS took a heavy battering, and in some areas a number of battalions were totally wiped out along with their commanders. Over the next few days the Allies continued to strike out, smashing into the 12.SS lines and causing massive damage to their positions. In the days leading up to July, the British, endeavouring to expand their bridgehead, became increasingly incensed at the conduct of the *Hitlerjugend* Division, who fought so tenaciously when their cause was so clearly lost. This dogged determination had managed to finally blunt the EPSOM operation, which consequently prevented it from acquiring the high plain south of Caen. Yet despite this success the division was badly depleted and its survivors exhausted. Most of the German forces around the city were in desperate need of being replenished.

Elsewhere in the area I and II Panzer Corps continued their counteroffensive. The *Frundsberg* Division fought for the town of Vieux, while its sister division *Hohenstaufen* attacked in the Baron region. *Hohenstaufen* fought a number of successful engagements and from 28 June to 1 July it scored no fewer than sixty-two Churchill II and III and Sherman tanks. However, in spite of this the attacks did not achieve any tactical success and casualties sustained by the division were also high with some 1,800 men killed or injured. The division's commander, *Standartenführer* Stadler, who assumed command on 3 July, reported the following regarding the fighting in Normandy:

> With every attack repelled, the confidence of the troops grew stronger, whereas the enemy's aggressive spirit seemed to decrease more and more. Although his attacks were always preceded by heavily massed artillery barrages lasting for hours, his tanks and infantrymen advanced only hesitatingly and very carefully and having suffered some casualties or losses, immediately turned around to have the artillery go into action again. The latter then even increased its intensity of fire, if a further intensification was at all possible. During those days, the enemy artillery fire reached such a pitch that veterans of the First World War unanimously agree, it surpassed even the fire in the trenches during the tremendous battles of matériel during the war.

Around Caen fighting still raged with the *Hitlerjugend*, foiling Allied attempts to break through its overstretched and depleted lines. As for the *Leibstandarte* and *Das Reich*, they had been put into action to prevent an enemy breakthrough into the French heartlands that were attempting to advance eastwards.

On 5 July, news reached Army Group B that Hitler contemplated having the *Hitlerjugend* relieved. However, three days later the SS Division was once again fighting another battle for Caen, code-named by the Allies as Operation CHARNWOOD.

Once again Meyer's 'boys' were the core of the defence and fought out the battle in the ruins around Caen with an aura suggesting that they were indestructible, even though their ranks had been decimated after weeks of continued defence. As the battle reached its peak, Hitler ordered the city to be held at all costs. However, with no more reserves left and ammunition rapidly running out, Meyer ordered the withdrawal of the division and instructed them to take a new defensive position in the rear.

By 11 July the *Hitlerjugend* was relieved by the *Leibstandarte*, which took command of two units that remained in action. For almost a week the *Leibstandarte* battled in the Caen region in a desperate attempt to stem the advancing Allies. On 18 July the British launched their second offensive, Operation GOODWOOD. This was an advance by three armoured divisions with the main objective of capturing the high ground north of Caen, and weakening *Panzergruppen* West so as to allow the American Operation COBRA to break out along the Cotentin peninsula.

Operation COBRA began with a massive combined aerial and ground bombing attack that saw some of the *Leibstandarte* units suffering severe losses. However, this did not discourage the SS soldiers, and still under the constant hammer blows of enemy artillery and anti-tank fire, the Panzers of *Leibstandarte* and the 21 Panzer Division moved forward to counterattack, supported by grenadiers huddled behind the hulls for protection. For this counterattack the SS could only muster forty-six armoured fighting vehicles and some self-propelled guns, but these were formed into a powerful two-pronged assault. Within hours of the counterattack the Germans had successfully thrown back the British spearheads. The latter lost more than 200 tanks, while between them the Germans lost 109 tanks, but the line had held.

The following day on 19 July the British attacked again, and at Bras in a fierce hand-to-hand battle annihilated a complete *Leibstandarte* grenadier battalion. On 20 July a Canadian Corps attacked the important Vassieres ridge and smashed through the 272nd Infantry Division behind which the *Leibstandarte* was in reserve. SS grenadiers fought a desperate close-quarter action, which saw both sides sustaining terrible casualties. Although later that day Operation GOODWOOD was called off, both the British and Canadians continued to keep seven of the remaining nine Panzer divisions occupied in the Caen sector. Six divisions of the American First and Third Armies had meanwhile moved south on the western side of the Cherbourg peninsula. The only German armoured divisions in their path were *Das Reich* and *Götz von Berlichingen*.

On 29 July the combined forces of *Das Reich* and *Götz von Berlichingen* attacked American forces near Saint-Denis-le-Gast, but the attack was soon suppressed by overwhelming Allied numerical superiority. On the same day the British launched Operation BLUECOAT, an assault in the direction of Vire on the boundary between the American and British forces. During this critical period the German Army Group quickly brought all available Panzer units from south of Caen to deal with the enemy threat. On 2 August, following heavy fighting, Vire was entered by the British but was quickly recaptured by two SS Panzer divisions the next day.

All over the Normandy sector the Waffen-SS divisions continued desperately trying to keep the Allies in check. The Norman countryside had created conditions that favoured the SS grenadiers. Clusters of trees, tall hedges, ditches and lack of roads frustrated the Allied armoured units seeking to destroy enemy tanks in open areas. Aided by this terrain, the SS were able to defend positions longer than the Allies had expected possible and as a result they incurred huge casualties. Frequently the Allies watched their irrepressible foe come under a furious crescendo of mortar and shellfire, and still they held their ground to the grim death. However, the savage Allied air attacks and naval bombardments gradually began to grind down the German defences. Movement was almost impossible by daylight and any vehicles that travelled during the day were attacked and destroyed.

By the end of the first week of August both the Wehrmacht and Waffen-SS divisions were fighting for survival. Corps and divisions remained in action on paper but were becoming a small collection of small battles, shrinking down to battalion size. A catastrophe now threatened the whole area as the Americans began to break out and the Normandy campaign became mobile. To save the German forces in Normandy from being completely encircled and destroyed, a series of rapid withdrawals was undertaken through the Falaise-Argentan gap. On 16 August German forces continued retreating and crossed the River Orne. The *Hitlerjugend* Division desperately fought to keep the gap open. The bulk of the German armour, however, that had become trapped inside the pocket at Falaise fought a desperate battle to escape the impending slaughter. By 21 August the terrible fighting in what became famously known as the Battle of the Falaise Pocket drew to a catastrophic conclusion. The Waffen-SS had been dealt a heavy blow and the battle for Normandy was lost.

(**Opposite, above**) Two camouflaged Panther Ausf.G tanks operating in France. The SS often used Panther tanks in France to ambush positions in woods and scored a high kill rate against Allied armour. Although the Panthers were virtually wiped out in Normandy, their units conducted bitter offensive and then defensive fighting, often holding back the enemy for some time.

(**Opposite, below**) During an enemy contact inside a French village a soldier can be seen here throwing an M1924 stick grenade.

Four photographs taken in sequence showing a battery of 15cm howitzers during a fire mission against an enemy target. This weapon was the standard artillery piece in a division and the employment of artillery was a necessity for any ground force engaging an enemy. Both infantry and motorized artillery regiments were still used extensively during this period of the war. It was very effective at clearing up heavily concentrated positions to let armour and infantry pour through unhindered. It was primarily designed to attack targets deep in the enemy's rear. This included command posts, reserve units, assembly areas and logistics facilities. *(NARA)*

(**Opposite, above**) Grenadiers during a lull in the fighting. While the soldiers sleep, one SS trooper can be seen cleaning his Karabiner 98k bolt-action rifle.

(**Above**) SS soldiers well concealed in undergrowth can be seen armed with their Karabiner 98k rifle, which was the standard issue weapon for all infantry during the war. Note that foliage has been attached to one of the soldiers' steel helmets to give him additional camouflage protection. *(NARA)*

(**Opposite, below**) Newly-decorated with the Iron Cross, this soldier ranked as an *SS-Hauptscharführer* can be seen here posing for the camera in front of a tent in a field during a lull in the fighting. *(NARA)*

(**Above**) A road sign reading 'Caen'. The area leading into the city was almost completely decimated following weeks of fighting. Fighting for the defence of Caen had not been without massive losses to both Waffen-SS and Wehrmacht soldiers. Yet despite the preparation of new defences to prevent an enemy offensive on the city, the 12th SS were in desperate need of replenishment of both men and equipment. *(Bender)*

(**Opposite, above**) Pictured in the middle here is *SS-Sturmbannführer* Kurt Meyer, the new divisional commander of the 12th SS. At only 33 years old, with Iron Cross, First and Second Class and the Knight's Cross with Oak Leaves, Meyer was the youngest divisional commander in the German armed forces. Out on the battlefield he was a daredevil commander of unorthodox methods and fought his battles deep inside enemy lines, but despite his skill and courageous character the change of command in the 12.SS made no tactical difference. In fact, he took command of the division with it being on the brink of disaster. Fighting for the defence of Caen had continued with massive losses, despite the preparation of new defences to prevent an enemy offensive on the city.

(**Opposite, below**) A Pz.Kpfw.IV belonging to SS-Panzer Regiment 12 of the 12th SS can be seen here stationary in a village. The authorized strength of SS-Panzer Regiment 12 consisted of 182 Panzers with 81 Pz.Kpfw.IVs or Panthers which were allocated to I *Abteilung*, while the remaining 101 Pz.Kpfw.IVs were allocated to II *Abteilung*.

An interesting photograph showing Tiger IIs parked inside a forest in July 1944. This was the first combat use of the Tiger II by the 1st Company of the 503rd Heavy Panzer Battalion, which saw it embroiled in action between Troarn and Démouville on 18 July. A week earlier, the battalion supported units of the *Leibstandarte* during Operation GOODWOOD.

Wehrmacht troops withdrawing through a village near Bayeux in late June. II SS Panzer Corps comprising the 9th SS Panzer Division *Hohenstaufen* and the 10th SS *Frundsberg* was to counterattack the British and Americans near Bayeux in order to drive a wedge between the two armies. However, this did not take place and instead, with supporting Wehrmacht units, the Germans fought a number of defensive actions.

Two photographs taken in sequence showing SS troops with captured British soldiers. Note the *SS-Feldgendarmerie* wearing the distinctive gorget. They wore the same uniform and gorget as their army counterparts, but had an additional cuff title indicating that they were military police. Generally they conducted the same policing role such as controlling rear areas, but they also undertook counter-insurgency measures against the local population.

(**Above**) A well-camouflaged Panther utilizing the side of a building to give it additional concealment against both enemy aerial and ground recognition. Note some grenadiers have hitched a lift on board the vehicle.

(**Right**) A photograph of *SS-Obersturmbannführer* Joachim Peiper who was given the command of SS-Panzer-Regiment.1 of the *Leibstandarte* during operations in Normandy. Peiper's regiment only saw action from 18 July. *(Bender)*

(**Opposite, above**) *Truppen* supported by a Panther tank move slowly along a typical Normandy road. This was known as hedge warfare, also known as the 'battle of the bocage'. The structure and layout of the hedges in Normandy was particularly unfavourable to the Allies. Both American and British forces rarely had sufficient views of the whole terrain, with the hedges often hiding lines of fire. They were also sometimes impassable and greatly impeded movement of platoons and combat groups. For the Germans, 'bocage' was a good natural ally.

(**Opposite, below**) A Panther belonging to the 12th SS Panzer Division *Hitlerjugend* near Caen in late June. On the morning of 26 June, an attack on Caen began code-named Operation EPSOM. During the day's fighting at least fifty enemy tanks were knocked out by Panthers, Pz.Kpfw.IVs and PaK guns alone. The 12th SS, however, took a heavy loss. In some areas a number of battalions were totally wiped out along with their commanders.

Three soldiers belonging to the 12th SS *Hitlerjugend* decorated for their bravery in action against British forces around Caen in June.

Soldiers from the 12th SS *Hitlerjugend* with a light MG 42 machine gun with extended bipod during operations in late June. Although a machine-gun troop was normally a three-man squad, due to the high casualty rates suffered on the Western Front they were commonly reduced to just two but were still highly effective. In Normandy the MG 42 machine gun proved its worth time and time again. The machine-gun crews constantly fought in close-quarter combat with the enemy but managed to stall them.

An SS soldier on the march. He is armed with the Karabiner 98k bolt-action rifle. Note the ammunition box attached to his back-straps.

A StuG.IV belonging to *Götz von Berlichingen* of *SS-Sturmgeschütz-Abteilung* 17. The division had forty-two of these vehicles in operation in the summer of 1944. Losses were high and remnants of the division were later temporarily assigned to the *Das Reich* Division and attached to XLVII Panzer Corps of the 7th Army.

Hitlerjugend soldiers being decorated following a successful engagement with British forces around Caen. *(BA/Bender)*

An SS soldier can be seen carrying a Teller mine. Teller mines were anti-tank devices that derived their name from the German word for 'plate', after the mine's flat, circular shape.

Two photographs showing the Nebelwerfer 42 in operation. There were several units in Normandy equipped with rocket artillery with the 21st Panzer Division containing the most batteries. The second photo is the *SS Nebeltruppen* of the 2nd *Werfer Batterie* of the *Leibstandarte* in July 1944 during a fire mission against an enemy target.

A Waffen-SS crew has utilized their 8.8cm FlaK gun against a ground target during heavy fighting. By 1944 the deadly 8.8cm FlaK gun was used extensively against both ground and aerial targets.

A 7.5cm PaK 40 during a fire mission. The weapon was effective against almost every Allied tank until the end of the war such as the American M4A3E2 Sherman, M26 Pershing and later variants of the British Churchill tank.

A mortar crew with the 8cm GW 34 mortar being prepared for a fire mission. This weapon remained the standard German infantry mortar throughout the war and gave the soldier valuable high-explosive capability beyond the range of rifles or grenades.

A 15cm gun with its crew can be seen in a field. The gun is being prepared for a fire mission.

(**Above**) A Panther Ausf.A advances along a track. Central to the German strategy of dealing with the Allies in Normandy was the use of strong, mobile armoured units such as the Tiger and Panther tanks. It came as a complete surprise when British and American tank crews found that the Panthers could often survive numerous hits, while a single round from one of their powerful 7.5cm guns was usually more than enough to destroy any enemy tank.

(**Opposite, above**) A light MG 42 gun squad rushes from one position to another inside a town that appears to have seen considerable fighting. Note the bipod of the machine gun is extended so that the gunner can quickly go into action with the weapon.

(**Opposite, below**) Soldiers taking refuge in a ravine during a lull in the fighting.

A Tiger from the 1st SS Panzer Regiment of the *Leibstandarte* can be seen here on the move in July 1944.

A soldier from the 12th SS can be seen here inside a Volkswagen 166. Behind him is a column of Panthers advancing through a town.

Epilogue

The Outcome

The Normandy campaign had been very costly for the Waffen-SS, with many of its elite units being annihilated. The *Leibstandarte* had suffered almost total destruction. *Das Reich* had some 450 men and 15 tanks remaining; *Hohenstaufen* had 460 men and some 25 tanks that had survived the slaughter. *Frundsberg* lost all of its tanks and artillery, while the *Hitlerjugend* had only 300 men remaining and no artillery. As for *Götz von Berlichingen*, it had been ordered to take part in the Mortain offensive, code-named Operation *LÜTTICH*. Following this failed offensive, the division was split into four *Kampfgruppen*: *Braune*, *Gunter*, *Fick* and *Wahl*. These small units were embroiled in heavy fighting in the Falaise Pocket and fought for their life trying to escape the slaughter. Most of the units did manage to escape encirclement but suffered heavy losses and remained in almost constant combat against the advancing Americans until the end of the month, when the division was transferred to Metz for a rest and refit.

As for the *Leibstandarte* it was withdrawn to Aachen, *Das Reich* limped back to the Schnee Eifel area, and the *Hitlerjugend* was pulled out and sent back east of Maas in Belgium. The *Hohenstaufen* and *Frundsberg* divisions were withdrawn to lick their wounds in a quiet backwater in Holland. Yet as they withdrew on 2 September, remnants of *Hohenstaufen*, now reduced to a *Kampfgruppe*, fought a successful defensive action at Cambrai, destroying more than forty enemy tanks. However, the division arrived in its new assembly area on 8 September almost decimated. It arrived near a town called Arnhem. Here on 10 September *Hohenstaufen* was ordered to turn over its remaining operational vehicles to its sister unit, the remnants of *Frundsberg*. Two grenadier battalions and an artillery battalion were also transferred. This left *Hohenstaufen* with only a cadre of approximately 2,500 men.

In spite of the almost total destruction of the Waffen-SS, the campaign had proved, as with the battles in the East, that they could delay the enemy but not defeat them.

Within months of the Normandy campaign the Waffen-SS would once again be refitted and ready for action. However, it was not to be another delaying action. This time the SS troops were to see action in Holland and in a bold and daring offensive through the Ardennes region. This was to be the Führer's last gamble in the West.

During a lull in the fighting an 8cm mortar crew can be seen here in a field. Their weapon has been camouflaged with saplings. This weapon was the principal infantry mortar used by both the Wehrmacht and Waffen-SS. Six were normally assigned to an infantry battalion's machine-gun company.

Two SS soldiers are seen here sheltering. By the end of July constant enemy aerial and ground bombardments persistently hindered infantry and armoured movements through Normandy. Often units had to take refuge inside forests and woods in order to help conceal themselves.

Travelling along a road and passing refugees is an Sd.Kfz.251/8 *Krankenpanzerwagen* which was outfitted and deployed as an armoured ambulance operating close to the front line. It was capable of carrying up to eight seated casualties or four seated casualties and two stretcher cases, and also the necessary first-aid and other medical equipment. *(BA/Bender)*

Inside a battle-scarred town children are seen playing on board a knocked-out Pz.Kpfw.IV. It appears that the extensive damage to the tank's side, which has blown off its side skirt, was the result of an enemy anti-tank gun.

Two knocked-out Panther tanks have been removed from the road and pushed into a ditch in the town of Saint-Lambert-sur-Dives in late August 1944. This town was the main German escape route eastwards between the towns of Chambois and Trun.

SS troops utilising bocage in the Norman countryside to conceal themselves. Bocage was terrain of mixed woodland and pasture characteristic of parts of Northern France. It was also referred to a small forest area too.

The carnage in the aftermath of Falaise. It was here around Falaise that the decisive battle of Normandy had been decided. German Army Group B, with the 7th Army and the 5th Panzer Army (formerly Panzer Group West) had been encircled by the Allies in what was known as the Falaise Gap or Pocket.

The aftermath of the destruction of the Falaise Pocket in late August 1944. The Battle of the Falaise Pocket ended the Battle of Normandy with a decisive German defeat. As for units of the Waffen-SS, they had shown minimal opposition as armour and troops desperately tried to escape the slaughter and withdrew across the River Seine.

The trail of devastation left by the Battle of Falaise. Dead horses, wagons and support elements of what was left of the German arsenal that did not escape the pocket is left in a long ditch strewn for miles.

A decimated Marder tank destroyer. The Battle of the Falaise Pocket had resulted in the destruction of Army Group B west of the Seine with some 450,000 German troops captured or killed. In the panic and confusion that preceded the army's annihilation, its remnants abandoned what heavy equipment they had left and escaped from the pocket, retreating eastwards to the German border. More than forty German divisions were destroyed during the Battle of Normandy. No exact figures are available, but it is estimated that the battle cost the German forces some 450,000 men, of whom 240,000 were killed or wounded.

Appendix

Order of Battle

1st Leibstandarte LAH

2nd SS Panzer Division *Das Reich*

9th SS-Panzer-Division *Hohenstaufen*

10th SS-Panzer-Division *Frundsberg*

12th SS Panzer Division *Hitlerjugend*

17th SS Panzergrenadier-Division *Götz von Berlichingen*

I SS Panzer Corps

1st Leibstandarte LAH

SS-Panzer-Grenadier-Regiment 1

Stab

I.Bataillon

1.Kompanie, 2.Kompanie, 3.Kompanie, 4.Kompanie, 5.Kompanie.

II.Bataillon

6.Kompanie, 7.Kompanie, 8.Kompanie, 9.Kompanie, 10.Kompanie.

III.Bataillon

11.Kompanie, 12.Kompanie, 13.Kompanie, 14.Kompanie, 15.Kompanie, 16.Flak-Kompanie, 17.Infanterie-Geschütz-Kompanie, 18.Panzerjäger-Kompanie, 19.Aufklärungs-Kompanie, 20.Pionier-Kompanie.

SS-Panzer-Grenadier-Regiment 2

Stab

I.Bataillon

1.Kompanie, 2.Kompanie, 3.Kompanie, 4.Kompanie, 5.Kompanie.

II.Bataillon

6.Kompanie, 7.Kompanie, 8.Kompanie, 9.Kompanie, 10.Kompanie.

III.Bataillon

11.Kompanie, 12.Kompanie, 13.Kompanie, 14.Kompanie, 15.Flak-Kompanie, 16.Infanteriegeschütz-Kompanie, 17.Panzerjäger-Kompanie, 18.Aufklärungs-Kompanie, 19.Pionier-Kompanie.

SS-Panzer-Aufklärungs-Abteilung 1

Stab

1.Kompanie, 2.Kompanie, 3.Kompanie, 4.Kompanie, 5.Kompanie, 6.Kompanie.

SS-Panzer-Regiment 1

Stab

I.Bataillon

1.Kompanie, 2.Kompanie, 3.Kompanie, 4.Kompanie.

II.Bataillon

5.Kompanie, 6.Kompanie, 7.Kompanie, 8.Kompanie, Schwhere Kompanie, Pionier-Kompanie.

SS-Panzerjäger-Abteilung

Stab

1.Kompanie, 2.Kompanie, 3.Kompanie.

SS-Sturmgeschütz-Abteilung

Stab

1.Kompanie, 2.Kompanie, 3.Kompanie.

SS-Panzer-Artillerie-Regiment

Stab

I.Abteilung

1.Batterie, 2.Batterie, 3.Batterie.

II.Abteilung

4.Batterie, 5.Batterie, 6.Batterie.

III.Abteilung

7.Batterie, 8.Batterie, 9.Batterie.

IV.Abteilung

10.Batterie, 11.Batterie, 12.Batterie.

SS-Flak-Abteilung 1

Stab

1.Kompanie, 2.Kompanie, 3.Kompanie, 4.Kompanie, 5.Kompanie, 2cm-Flak-Aug.

SS-Panzer-Pionier-Bataillon
Stab
1.Kompanie, 2.Kompanie, 3.Kompanie, 4.Kompanie.

SS-Panzer-Nachrichten-Abteilung
Stab
1.Kompanie, 2.Kompanie.

2nd SS Panzer Division Das Reich, 1944

SS-Panzer Regiment 2
I.Abteilung
1.Kompanie, 2.Kompanie, 3.Kompanie.
II.Abteilung
4.Kompanie, 5.Kompanie, 6.Kompanie.

SS Panzergrenadier Regiment Deutschland
I. Bataillon
1.Kompanie, 2.Kompanie, 3.Kompanie, 4.Kompanie.
II. Battalion
5.Kompanie, 6.Kompanie, 7.Kompanie, 8.Kompanie.
III. Bataillon
9.Kompanie, 10.Kompanie, 11.Kompanie, 12.Kompanie, 13.Kompanie.

SS Panzergrenadier Regiment Der Führer
I. Bataillon
1.Kompanie, 2.Kompanie, 3.Kompanie, 4.Kompanie.
II. Bataillon
5.Kompanie, 6.Kompanie, 7.Kompanie, 8.Kompanie.
III. Bataillon
9.Kompanie, 10.Kompanie, 11.Kompanie, 12.Kompanie, 13.Kompanie.

SS-Panzer Artillerie Regiment 2
I. Abteilung
1. Batterie, 2. Batterie, 3. Batterie.
II. Abteilung
4. Batterie, 5. Batterie, 6. Batterie.
III. Abteilung
7. Batterie, 8. Batterie, 9. Batterie.
IV. Abteilung
10. Batterie, 11. Batterie, 12. Batterie.
SS-Kradschützen Bataillon 2
1. Kompanie, 2. Kompanie, 3. Kompanie, 4. Kompanie, 5. Kompanie.

SS-Sturmgeschütz Abteilung 2
  1. Batterie, 2. Batterie, 3. Batterie.
SS-Aufklärungs Abteilung 2
  1. Kompanie, 2. Kompanie, 3. Kompanie, Leichte Aufklärungskolonne.
SS-Panzerjäger Abteilung 2
  1. Kompanie, 2. Kompanie, 3. Kompanie.
SS-Flak Abteilung 2.
  1. Batterie, 2. Batterie, 3. Batterie, 4. Batterie, 5. Batterie, Leichte Artillerie Kolonne
SS-Panzer Pionier Abteilung 2
  1. Kompanie, 2. Kompanie, 3. Kompanie, Brückenkolonne Leichte Pionier Kolonne.
SS-Nachrichten Abteilung 2
  1. Kompanie, 2. Kompanie, Leichte Nachrichten Kolonne.
SS-Wirtschafts Bataillon 2
  Verpflegungsamt Bäckerie Kompanie, Schlachterie Kompanie.
SS-Nachschubdienste 2
  1. Kraftwagenkolonne, 2. Kraftwagenkolonne, 3. Kraftwagenkolonne,
  4. Kraftwagenkolonne, 5. Kraftwagenkolonne, 6. Kraftwagenkolonne,
  7. Kraftwagenkolonne, 8. Kraftwagenkolonne, 9. Kraftwagenkolonne,
  10. Kraftwagenkolonne, 11. Kraftwagenkolonne, 12. Kraftwagenkolonne,
  13. Kraftwagenkolonne, 14. Kraftwagenkolonne, 15. Kraftwagenkolonne,
  Nachschubkompanie, Waffen Werkstattkompanie.
2. SS-Instandsetzungsdienst
  1. Werkstattkompanie, 2. Werkstattkompanie, 3. Werkstattkompanie,
  Ersatz Kolonne.
2. SS-Sanitätsabteilung
  Feldazarett, 1. Sanitatskompanie, 2. Sanitatskompanie, 1. Krankenkraftwagenzug,
  2. Krankenkraftwagenzug, 3. Krankenkraftwagenzug, Stabskompanie,
  Feldgendarmerie Truppe, Feldpostamt, SS-Kriegsberichter Zug 2.

9th SS-Panzer-Division Hohenstaufen

19.SS-Panzergrenadier-Regiment, 20.SS-Panzergrenadier-Regiment,
9.SS-Panzer-Regiment, 9.SS-Artillerie-Regiment, 9.SS-Aufklärung-Abteilung,
9.SS-Panzerjäger-Abteilung, 9.SS-Flak-Abteilung, 9.SS-Pionier-Abteilung,
9.SS-Panzer-Nachrichten-Abteilung, 9th SS Divisional Support Units.

10th SS-Panzer-Division Frundsberg

SS-Panzergrenadier-Regiment 21, SS-Panzergrenadier-Regiment 22,
SS-Panzer-Regiment 10, SS-Panzer-Artillerie-Regiment 10,
SS-Kradschützen-Regiment 10, SS Sturmgeschütz-Abteilung 10,
SS Panzerjäger-Abteilung 10, SS Flak-Abteilung 10, SS Pionier-Abteilung 10,

SS Panzer-Nachrichten-Abteilung 10, SS-Verwaltungs Truppen 10, SS-Instandsetzungs Abteilung 10, SS-Sanitäts-Abteilung 10, SS-Nachschub Truppen 10, SS-Feldpostamt 10, SS-Kriegsberichter-Zug 10, SS-Feldgendarmerie-Trupp 10.

12th SS Panzer Division Hitlerjugend

SS-Panzergrenadier Regiment 25, SS-Panzergrenadier Regiment 26, SS-Panzer Regiment 12, SS-Panzer Artillerie Regiment 12, SS-Kradschützen-Regiment 12, SS-Aufklärungs-Abteilung 12, SS-Kradschützen-Regiment 12, SS-Panzerjäger-Abteilung 12, SS-Werfer-Abteilung 12, SS-Flak-Abteilung 12, SS-Pionier-Abteilung 12, SS-Panzer-Nachrichten-Abteilung 12, SS-Instandsetzungs 12, SS-Nachschub-Truppen 12, SS-Wirtschafts-Bataillon 12, SS-Führerbewerber-Lehrgange, SS-Kriegsberichter-Zug (mot) 12, SS-Feldgendarmerie-Kompanie/Trupp 12, SS-Feldpostamt (mot) 12, SS-Sanitäts-Abteilung 12, SS-Werfer-Abteilung 12 (4).

SS Panzer Regiment 12 (tactical numbers)

Rgt. Stab: Rgt Kommandeur	055
Rgt Adjutant	054
Ordonnanz-Offz.	053
Aufklärungszug	056–060

I.Abteilung

Abt. Stab Kommandeur	155
Adjutant	154
Nachr.Offz	153
Aufklärungszug	156–160

I.Kp		2.Kp	
Kp.Führer	105	Kp.Führer	205
Kp.-Truppfhr	104	Kp.-Truppfhr	204
1.Zug/Zugf.	115	1.Zug/Zugf.	215
	116–119		216–219
2.Zug/Zugf.	125	2.Zug/Zugf.	225
	126–129		226–229
3.Zug/Zugf.	135	3.Zug/Zugf.	235
	136–139		236–239
4.Zug/Zugf.	145	4.Zug/Zugf.	245
	146–149		246–249

3.Kp	
Kp.Führer	305
Kp.-Truppfhr	304
1.Zug/Zugf.	315
	316–319
2.Zug/Zugf.	325
	326–329
3.Zug/Zugf.	335
	336–339
4.Zug/Zugf.	345
	346–349

4.Kp	
Kp.Führer	405
Kp.-Truppfhr	404
1.Zug/Zugf.	415
	416–419
2.Zug/Zugf.	425
	426–429
3.Zug/Zugf.	435
	436–439
4.Zug/Zugf.	445
	446–449

II.Abteilung

Abt. Stab Kommandeur	555
Adjutant	554
Nachr.Offz	553
Aufklärungszug	556–560

5.Kp	
Kp.Führer	505
Kp.-Truppfhr	504
1.Zug/Zugf.	515
	516–519
2.Zug/Zugf.	525
	526–529
3.Zug/Zugf.	535
	536–539
4.Zug/Zugf.	545
	546–549

6.Kp	
Kp.Führer	605
Kp.-Truppfhr	604
1.Zug/Zugf.	615
	616–619
2.Zug/Zugf.	625
	626–629
3.Zug/Zugf.	635
	636–639
4.Zug/Zugf.	645
	646–649

7.Kp	
Kp.Führer	705
Kp.-Truppfhr	704
1.Zug/Zugf.	715
	716–719
2.Zug/Zugf.	725
	726–729
3.Zug/Zugf.	735
	736–739
4.Zug/Zugf.	745
	746–749

8.Kp	
Kp.Führer	805
Kp.-Truppfhr	804
1.Zug/Zugf.	815
	816–819
2.Zug/Zugf.	825
	826–829
3.Zug/Zugf.	835
	836–839
4.Zug/Zugf.	845
	846–849

17th SS Panzergrenadier-Division Götz von Berlichingen

37th SS-Panzergrenadier-Regiment
38th SS-Panzergrenadier-Regiment
17th SS-Panzer Battalion, 17th SS Artillerie Regiment, 17th SS-Panzerjäger Battalion, 17th SS-Sturmgeschütz Battalion, 17th SS Flak Battalion, 17th SS Signal Battalion, 17th SS Panzer Reconnaissance Battalion, 17th SS-Pionier Battalion, 17th SS-Division-Nachschub-Truppen, 17th SS-Panzer Instandsetzungs Battalion (Maintenance Battalion), 17th SS-Wirtschaft Battalion, 17th SS Medical Battalion.

I.SS Panzer Corps

Main Divisions:
101st SS Heavy Panzer Battalion, 1st SS Panzer Division Leibstandarte, 12th SS Panzer Division Hitlerjugend, 17th SS Division Götz von Berlichingen, Panzer-Lehr Division.
General Composition:
Fliegerstaffel, SS-Korpskartenstelle Schwere, SS-Panzerabteilung 101/501, SS-Artillerie-Kommandeur I, SS-Artillerie-Abteilung 101/501, SS-Flugabwehrkanone-Abteilung 101, SS-Flugabwehr-Kompanie, SS-Wefer-Abteilung 101/501, SS-Vielfachwerferbatterie (mot) 101/501, SS-Korps-Nachrichten-Abteilung 101/501, Schwere SS-Beobachtungsbatterie 101/501, SS-Wehrgeologen-Bataillon 101, SS-Korps-Nachstub-Truppen 101, SS-Kraftfahr-Kompanie 101, SS-Korps-Sanitäts-Abteilung 101, SS-Feldlazarett 501, SS-Krankenkraftwagen-Zug 501, SS-Feldpostamt (mot) 101 (Field Post Office), SS-Kriegsberichter-Kompanie (mot), SS-Feldgendarmerie-Kompanie 101 (mot), SS-Korps-Sicherungs-Kompanie 101.

II.SS Panzer Corps

Main Divisions:
102nd SS Heavy Panzer Battalion, 9th SS-Panzer-Division Hohenstaufen, 10th SS-Panzer-Division Frundsberg.
General Composition:
Fliegerstaffel SS-Korpskartenstelle (mot) 102, Schwere SS-Panzerabteilung 102/502, SS-Artillerie-Kommandeur II, SS-Artillerie-Abteilung 102, SS-Granatwefer-Kompanie 102, SS-Flugabwehr-Kompanie 102, SS-Wefer-Abteilung 102, SS-Korps-Nachrichten Abteilung 400, SS-Wehrgeologen-Kompanie 102, SS-Kraftfährzeug-Instand-Setzungs Kompanie 102, SS-Werkstatt-Kompanie 102, SS-Korps-Sanitäts-Kompanie 102.

Notes